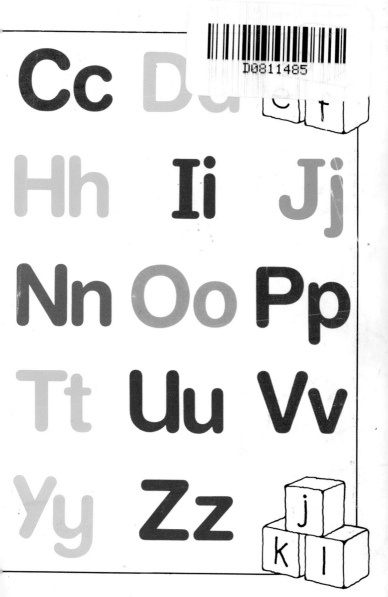

Learning Points

*This simple, colourful book helps children to learn to
recognise the letters of the alphabet by pairing each
letter with an appealing, familiar object.*

- As you look at the book together, encourage your
  child to say the sound of the letter rather than it's name
  (that is, **a** as in *apple* rather than **a** as in *age*).

- Talk about the pictures – does she like apples?
  Where has he seen an elephant? What are the colours
  on the parrot's wing?

- Play I-spy at home and on trips out. Remember to use
  the letter sound.

Acknowledgment

The publishers would like to thank GCP Ltd for supplying the
soft letters used on the cover of this book.

Produced exclusively for
ASDA Stores Ltd
Great Wilson Street
Leeds LS11 5AD
by Ladybird Books Ltd
27 Wrights Lane London
W8 5TZ

©Ladybird Books Ltd

alphabet

illustrated by Liz Antill

ASDA
play and learn

a

apple

b

ball

cat

d

duck

e

elephant

f

fish

goat

h

house

ink

jam

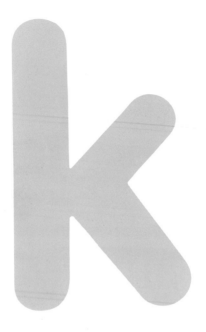

kite

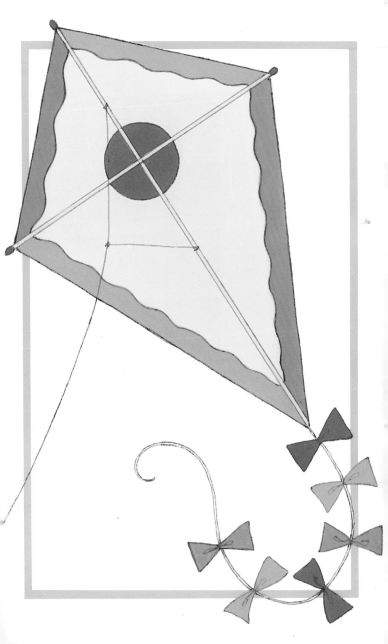

ladder

m

mouse

n

nest

o

orange

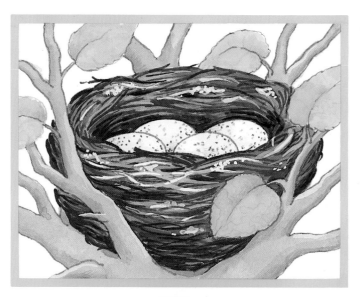

p

parrot

queen

r

rainbow

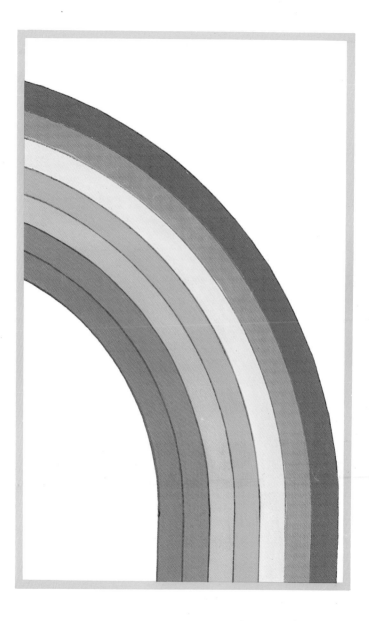

S

sun

t

tiger

u

umbrella

V

violin

W

watch

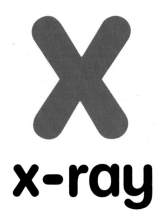

x-ray

x as in box

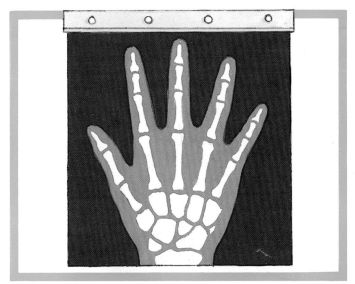

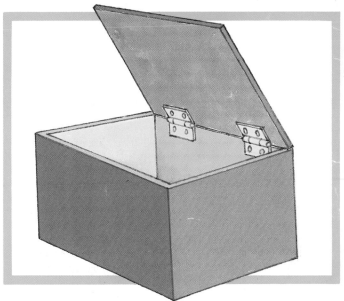

y

yo-yo

z

zebra